FOREWORD

Hi!

This is the story on how I got started on this project.

I am a Gujarati girl from Malacca with a distinctly Malaysian palate who married into a vegetarian South Indian family who take their food seriously. When I first started cooking, I had no culinary skills. I regularly browsed through recipe books looking for inspiration. The pictures in these books would look appetizing and the dishes sounded delicious, but most of the time, I was disappointed as I found the recipes too complicated or the ingredients would be hard to come by.

My journey to creating culinary delights began when we formed a singing group. Every month, fourteen of us would gather in one of our homes to practice our crooning skills and treat ourselves to food that the host had prepared.

At the end of the session we would discuss the recipes of the food we had eaten and then go on to discuss other recipes. All of us felt a need for good, nutritious food that was easy to make, using simple ingredients. That was when I decided to work on this compilation.

In this book, I have tried to keep my recipes simple using ingredients that are readily available. My objective is to put together a variety of uncomplicated, yet delicious recipes that is a beginning to easy cooking.

Try these lip smacking recipes from my kitchen tonight and I hope they give as much pleasure to you and your families as they have to me and mine.

Varsha S Patel

Recipes From My Home Kitchen

Varsha S. Patel

Library of Congress Control Number:		2013908525
ISBN:	Hardcover	978-1-4836-3881-2
	Softcover	978-1-4836-3880-5
	Ebook	978-1-4836-3882-9

Rev. date: 05/20/2013

To order additional copies of this book, contact:
Xlibris Corporation
1-800-618-969
www.Xlibris.com.au
Orders@Xlibris.com.au
503133

CONTENTS

APPETIZERS

Whenever I have guests for dinner, a most important ritual is 'ice-breaking'. I make my guests as comfortable as possible to ensure that the party kicks off on the right note. The importance of an appetizer here therefore, cannot be underestimated.

A good appetizer would give your guests something to talk about, and whet their appetite while they are waiting for the main course.

But remember, not too much of the appetizer as this could ruin your guests' appetite for the main meal.

SALSA WITH NACHOS

This is a simple yet a great appetizer, which can be eaten with Nacho chips.

Ingredients

2 tomatoes
2 big onions
2 pips garlic
2 red chillies

2 – 3 tablespoons chopped fresh coriander leaves
juice from 1 big lime
salt to taste
¼ teaspoon pepper, roughly pounded

1. Chop the above ingredients into small pieces
2. Add lime juice, pepper and salt to taste. Mix well and the salsa is ready.

MUSHROOM ON TOAST

This dish is a light snack that is ideal for tea parties. I first tasted this dish at a friend's place and I immediately fell in love with it.

Ingredients

1 can button mushroom or 12
    fresh button mushrooms, cut
    into small pieces.
75 g butter
2 medium sized onions, finely
    chopped

1 ½ cups milk
2 teaspoons corn flour
2 tablespoons whipping
    cream
salt to taste
¼ teaspoon pepper

Method:

1. Heat butter in a wok.
2. Once the butter has melted, add the onions and fry till the onions turn golden brown.
3. Add in the chopped mushrooms and fry for 5 more minutes, stirring occasionally.
4. Then add in the milk, salt, pepper and also corn flour. Stir well until the mixture thickens.
5. Add in the whipped cream and stir for 2 more minutes.
6. The dish is done. Serve hot with buttered toast.

Note: if you have a toaster oven, you may grill the bread topped with mushrooms for 2 minutes. Make sure the bread is covered with a generous layer of mushroom sauce before grilling.

SPLIT PEAS DAL SALAD (KOS MOORI)

This is a popular dish that I had the pleasure of tasting when I was in Bangalore (India) while visiting my husband's relatives. While this dish is usually made in conjunction with religious festivals, it is very healthy and makes a great snack.

Ingredients:

Main Ingredients:

1 cup split peas dal (Mung dal)

1 medium sized cucumber, peeled and chopped into small pieces

1 tablespoon grated coconut

2 green chillies finely chopped

¼ cup fresh coriander leaves, finely chopped

12 curry leaves, finely chopped

juice of 1 lime

salt to taste

For seasoning:

¼ teaspoon mustard seeds

2 dry chillies

1 tablespoon oil

A pinch of asafoetida powder (hing)

Method:

1. Soak the mung dal for about 45 minutes. Then wash and drain.
2. Add cucumber, grated coconut, green chillies, coriander leaves and curry leaves together with the mung dal in a bowl.

3. Now add salt and lime juice. Mix well. Keep it aside.
4. Heat oil in a wok.
5. Once the oil is heated, add the asafoetida powder, mustard seeds and dry chillies. Once the mustard seeds start crackling add this to the main ingredients.
6. Mix well and it is ready to be eaten.

Mung dal can be substituted with split chick peas (chana dal).

CORNFLAKES MIXTURE

Ingredients

1 big box of Kellogg's cornflakes
200 g yellow raisins
200 g cashews
500 g peanuts

100 g almonds, chopped into small pieces
Lots of dry chillies
A fist of curry leaves
salt to taste
1 teaspoon sugar
½ tablespoon chilli powder
oil for deep frying

Spices (Garam Masala Mix)
    1 whole nutmeg
    3 sticks dry ginger
    5 sticks cinnamon
    1 fist cardamom
    ¼ teaspoon clove
    1 teaspoon pepper

Method:

1. Pound or grind altogether the spices (Garam Masala Mix) until it resembles a fine powder.
2. Deep fry the cornflakes in a wok for not more than 5 seconds. Don't fry for too long, or the cornflakes will burn. Put all the fried cornflakes into a big pot.

3. Next fry the peanuts till they become crunchy. Add the peanuts to the cornflakes.
4. Similarly fry the cashews, almonds, curry leaves and dry chillies separately and keep adding them into the pot with the fried cornflakes.
5. Finally fry the raisins and add in the pot.
6. Now add the homemade "garam masala mix", salt, sugar, and chilli powder into the pot and mix well.
7. You can adjust the mixture to be sweeter, saltier or spicier to suit your palate.

A
NORTH INDIAN
MEAL

In this section, I am providing an assortment of easy to make yet tasty dishes which have a distinctly North Indian flavour.

These dishes can be served with either bread or rice. The most common of the bread types are the chapatti and the poori, both of which need no introduction to Indians.

Alternatively, the "Biryani" or the "Pulao" are popular rice dishes with which these vegetables can be served.

As the above rice and bread dishes are well known to most Malaysians, I have provided the recipes for three lesser known dishes that can be eaten with vegetables accompaniments.

NORTH INDIAN VEGETABLES

MUSHROOM BUTTER MASALA

Ingredients

1 can button mushroom, quartered

½ cup natural yoghurt

½ teaspoon turmeric

2 teaspoons garam masala

1 teaspoon ground cumin

2 teaspoons fresh ginger, finely pounded

2 pips garlic, pounded

10 cashews

2 tablespoons butter

1 tablespoon oil

1 onion, finely chopped

1 teaspoon ground cardamom

1 cinnamon stick

1 teaspoon chilli powder

3 tablespoons tomato puree

150 ml vegetable stock

1 cup double/thickened cream

1 teaspoon lemon juice

salt to taste

Method:

1. Combine mushroom, yoghurt, lemon juice, garam masala, chilli powder, cumin, ginger and garlic in a bowl. Mix well and keep aside for 10 min.
2. Grind the cashews into a powder and keep aside.
3. Heat the butter and oil in a wok over medium heat. Add the cinnamon and onions. Fry the onions till they become transparent. Now add tomato puree, cashew powder, marinated mushroom, salt and stock. Simmer for 15 minutes.
4. Now add the cream and cook for a further 10 minutes over a low flame and the dish is done.

Note: I find that the "Everest Garam Masala" gives my cooking the best taste. Fresh mushrooms can be used instead of the canned variety. The dish also works well with cottage cheese ("paneer") instead of mushrooms.

GARLIC POTATO (LASAN ALOO)

Ingredients

3 potatoes, to be cut into
   wedges
1½ tablespoons chilli powder
salt to taste
5 tablespoons oil

Pound in mortar with pestle:
1 tablespoon cumin seeds
3 pips garlic

Method:

1. Heat oil in a wok.
2. Add potatoes, cover the wok and let it cook for 5 minutes over a low flame to prevent the potatoes from burning.
3. Once the potatoes are half cooked, add the pounded garlic and cumin seeds, chilli powder and salt. Mix well and cover again.
4. Simmer over a low flame until the potatoes are cooked. Remember to stir the potatoes occasionally so that the potatoes get cooked evenly.

RED KIDNEY BEANS CURRY (RAJMA)

Ingredients

2 tablespoons clarified butter (ghee)

2 onions, chopped roughly

2 medium tomatoes

1 tablespoon chilli powder

½ cup water

1 can red kidney beans, rinse under tap (discard liquid in tin)

¼ teaspoon coriander powder

¼ teaspoon cumin powder

salt to taste

2 tablespoons oil

Method:

1. Heat oil in a wok. Add the onions and fry till the onions become transparent.
2. Add the tomatoes and fry till the tomatoes soften. Switch off the stove. Keep the wok aside for a few minutes to let the mixture cool and blend the mixture into a paste.
3. Heat clarified butter in the same wok and then add in the ground paste. Let it cook for 3 minutes.
4. Add in the kidneys beans, chilli powder, salt and coriander and cumin powder. Mix well and let it cook for another 3 minutes.
5. Add in water and stir well. Let it cook for 5 minutes over a low flame. Taste the curry. Add more water and salt if required.

Serve it hot with any Indian bread or rice.

Note:

Cumin and coriander powder mix can be bought from any Indian grocery shop. It is called Dhana Jeera powder. I use the mix instead of using the 2 powders separately.

Fresh kidney beans can also be used. The beans will have to be soaked overnight and then cooked in the pressure cooker to soften them.

TOMATO CURRY

Ingredients

3 tomatoes

2 pips garlic, pounded

¼ teaspoon cumin seeds

¼ teaspoon mustard seeds

¼ teaspoon turmeric powder

½ tablespoon chilli powder

¼ teaspoon sugar

½ glass water

salt to taste

2 tablespoons oil

Method:

1. Heat oil in a wok and add in cumin seeds, mustard seeds and garlic. Fry for 1 minute.
2. Add in tomatoes and fry till soft
3. Add salt, sugar, turmeric powder and chilli powder and stir well.
4. Add ½ a glass water and let it to boil for 5 minutes over a medium flame.
5. Serve with rice or Indian bread.

POTATO PEAS CURRY (ALOO MUTTER)

Ingredients

2 to 3 onions

2 big tomatoes

1 pip garlic (optional)

1 tablespoon Garam Masala

1 tablespoon Pav Bhaji Masala

3 potatoes, cubed into small
   pieces.

1 cup frozen green peas

¼ teaspoon mustard seeds

¼ teaspoon cumin seeds

a pinch of asafoetida

salt to taste

2 tablespoons oil

2 tablespoons chopped
   coriander leaves

Method:

1. Heat oil in a deep wok and add the mustard seeds. Fry till the seeds crackle.
2. Add the cumin seeds, asafoetida and garlic.
3. Add in the onions and fry till transparent.
4. Add in the tomatoes, green peas and potatoes.
5. Add in half a cup water and cover the wok. Ensure the flame is on medium setting and cook till the potatoes are soft. Add in more water if required.
6. Once potatoes are soft, add in both the garam masala and pav bhaji masala
7. Add salt and a pinch of sugar. Stir well and simmer for 2 minutes.
8. Add more water to get a thinner consistency if preferred. My preference is for a thick consistency.
9. Add the coriander leaves and boil for another 5 minutes.

VEGETABLE KURMA

Ingredients

vegetables of your choice	5 onions
2 tomatoes	1 teaspoon of garam masala
1 slice of ginger	1 glass of yoghurt
3 tablespoons chopped coriander leaves	2 green chillies
	salt to taste
2 tablespoons of tomato puree	2 tablespoons oil
4 teaspoons of coriander and cumin powder mix (Dhana Jeera Powder)	

For this particular recipe, you may use any vegetable of your choice—potatoes, carrot, cauliflower or frozen green peas. Boil vegetables required separately and keep aside.

Method:

1. Cut onions, chillies and tomatoes in cubes.
2. Heat oil in a wok and add the onions and ginger.
3. Fry onions until it becomes transparent then add the tomatoes and chillies. Fry till the tomatoes soften. Keep aside and let it cool.
4. Once cooled, blend the above ingredients together with the coriander leaves, the powders, yoghurt, chillies and tomato puree into a smooth paste.

5. Put the blended paste back into the same wok. Fry the paste for 5 minutes over a medium flame then add the boiled vegetables.
6. Add ½ a cup water, salt and a pinch of sugar. If it is too thick, add more water as required.
7. Simmer for another 2 minutes and your curry is done.

NORTH INDIAN BREAD

BHATURA

Ingredients

2 cups white flour (Maida)

2 to 3 cups yoghurt

1/3 cup suji/semolina (rava)

2 tablespoons oil

½ teaspoon sugar

oil for deep frying

salt to taste

Note: This recipe is for 2 persons. (5 cups of maida and 1 cup suji is required for 4 to 5 persons)

Method:

1. Mix all the above ingredients well and knead with yoghurt. Do not use any water. Knead well and ensure dough is not soft.
2. Make even balls (table tennis ball size) and keep aside.
3. Roll each ball flat separately with a rolling pin. If the dough starts to stick to the rolling pin add a little plain flour to the rolled dough. Make sure the dough rolled out is flat and thin.
4. Heat up oil for frying in a deep frying pan or wok.
5. Once the oil is really hot, cook the bhatura one by one.
6. The bhatura should be cooked evenly on both sides. The colour of the bhatura should be light brown/golden.
7. Drain the bhatura on paper towel to get rid of the excess oil.

Bhatura can be eaten with any of the vegetable recipes in this section, but it is more popularly served with chick pea curry.

NORTH INDIAN RICE

TOMATO RICE

Ingredients

1 cup rice

1 clove garlic, chopped into
small pieces

2 to 3 onions, chopped into
small pieces

1 small tin of tomato puree

¼ teaspoon cumin seeds

1 cinnamon stick

salt to taste

2 tablespoons oil

¼ teaspoon turmeric powder

½ teaspoon cumin and
coriander seeds powder
mix (dhana jeera powder)

Method:

1. Heat oil in a wok. Add cumin seeds, cinnamon stick, onions and garlic. Fry till onions become slightly brown and transparent.
2. Add the washed rice, turmeric powder, cumin and coriander seeds powder mix. Stir well, then add salt and tomato puree.
3. Stir well then put the mixture into a rice cooker.

Tomato rice can be served with pickle and yoghurt salad (raita).

Note: Water for the rice is according to your rice requirement.
I use a 1:2 proportion of rice to water.

ONION FRIED RICE (WAZIR PULAO)

Ingredients

4 big onions, cut length wise

3 teaspoons chilli powder

2 cups cooked rice

1 cinnamon stick

salt to taste

6 tablespoons oil

Method:

1. Add the chilli powder and salt to the rice. Mix well and keep aside.
2. Now in a wok, heat oil and add the cinnamon stick.
3. Next add the onions, fry them till they become dark brown.
4. Add in the rice, mix well and fry for 3 minutes.

SOUTH INDIAN
MEAL

Being married into a Brahmin family from Kerala has given me an opportunity to experience a whole new world of culinary experiences.

My exposure to this type of cooking was limited till then. It was only after my marriage that I realised that there were many different types of Sambar, Rasam and Pachadis till my father-in law, who is himself an excellent cook, explained to me the intricacies of this dish.

It was quite difficult at first for me to grasp this type of complexity but once I went into the details, the mix of flavours is actually quite simple. While I thought some of the dishes were bland initially, I learnt that these were served with spicy accompaniments to complete the meal.

I have therefore tried in this section, to furnish the details of a few typical South Indian dishes in a manner that is simple to understand and yet easy to make.

In a South Indian meal, rice forms the staple dish around which all other accompaniments are centered. As an alternative to rice, the "thosai" (which is also rice based) makes a marvelous change.

SOUTH INDIAN ACCOMPANIMENTS

SAMBAR

Ingredients

2 big tomatoes

tamarind juice (1 lemon size
  ball mixed with 1 glass of
  water)

¼ teaspoon turmeric powder
  (heldi)

2 – 3 tablespoons sambar
  powder (recipe provided)

6 pieces curry leaves

3 tablespoons coriander leaves

½ tablespoon sugar

100g pigeon peas (Tuvar Dal)

a pinch of asafoetida (hing)

salt to taste

vegetable of choice: potatoes,
  okra, carrots, white radish
  and egg plant

Ingredients for Seasoning

2 –3 dry chillies

½ teaspoon black gram (urad dal)

½ teaspoon split chick peas
  (chana dal)

½ teaspoon mustard seeds

¼ teaspoon fenugreek seeds

2 tablespoons oil or clarified
  butter (ghee)

Method for the Sambar

1. Pressure-cook or boil 100g tuvar dhal with 2 full cups of water.
   Once done churn the dal till it froths and keep it aside.

2. Take a medium size pot and add the tamarind juice, tomatoes, asafoetida, turmeric powder, curry leaves and one teaspoon salt to begin. Also add the vegetables of your choice.
3. Boil till the tomatoes and vegetables are soft and add the prepared tuvar dal and boil for 5 minutes.
4. Add the sambar powder and sugar. Stir well
5. Boil for another 2 minutes. Taste the sambar. Add more salt if required.
6. Once done add the seasoning and garnish with coriander leaves.

Method for seasoning:

Heat clarified butter or oil in a small wok. Once hot add all the ingredients for seasoning. Once the mustard seeds begin to crackle, pour this mixture into the main sambar pot. I prefer to use clarified butter (ghee) in my seasoning as I find it enhances the flavour of the sambar.

SAMBAR POWDER

Ingredients

½ cup black gram (urad dal)

3 cups coriander seeds

¼ cup split chick peas (chana dal)

¼ cup pigeon peas (tuvar dal)

½ teaspoon fenugreek seeds

½ teaspoon mustard seeds

¾ tablespoon cumin seeds

¾ tablespoon whole black pepper

1 teaspoon asafoetida

3 cups chilli powder

Method:

Roast all the above ingredients in the following order for 5 minutes (without oil) over a medium heat. You start off with

1. Black gram (urad dal)
2. After 1 minute add the split chick peas (chana dal) and pigeon peas (tuvar dal).
3. A minute later add the cumin seeds, fenugreek seeds, mustard seeds, pepper and asafoetida.
4. After another minute add in the coriander seeds.

Continue to roast. Once the mix becomes fragrant, turn off the stove and keep it aside. Let the mixture cool down. Then add the chilli powder. Mix well.

Grind the above into fine powder. Your sambar power is ready. Make sure the powder is stored in an airtight container to ensure the flavours are retained.

Note: you may use this powder for making rasam.

RASAM

Ingredients

2 big tomatoes
tamarind juice
(approximately 1 lemon
size ball mixed with 1 ½
glass of water)
¼ teaspoon turmeric
powder
1 ½ tablespoons sambar
powder/rasam powder
(readily available)
6 curry leaves

3 tablespoons chopped
coriander leaves
A small fistful of pigeon
peas (tuvar dal)
salt to taste
a pinch of asafoetida

Ingredients for the Seasoning

2 –3 dry chillies
½ teaspoon black gram
(urad dal)
½ teaspoon split chick peas
(chana dal)

½ teaspoon mustard seeds
¼ teaspoon fenugreek seeds
2 tablespoons oil or
clarified butter (ghee)

Method:

1. Pressure cook or boil a small fistful (about 50g) of pigeon peas
   dal in 2 glasses of water till it is a watery pulp.

2. Take a medium size pot and add the tamarind juice, tomatoes, turmeric powder, curry leaves and one teaspoon of salt to begin with.
3. Boil till the tomatoes become soft.
4. Now add the rasam powder or sambar powder for 2 minutes.
5. Now add the pigeon peas pulp and boil for another 3 minutes.
6. Taste the rasam. Add more sambar/rasam powder to get the right level of spice for you and more salt if required.
7. While the rasam is boiling, season the rasam in a similar method to the sambar and add the chopped coriander leaves.

Rasam can be eaten with rice, thosai or by itself as a soup. You could also use MTR Rasam powder as a substitute for the sambar powder.

Note:

If you're having a cold or sore throat, add ½ teaspoon crushed pepper and 2 to 3 pips of garlic in stage 2. Drink it while it is hot, with a little ghee. It will help to relieve the problem.

It is best to use lentils from India for your sambar and rasam and these are easily obtained from your local Indian grocery store. This type of lentil cooks faster and lends a better flavour to the rasam.

ONION AND TOMATO CHUTNEY

Ingredients

3 big onions   salt to taste
2 big tomatoes   A pinch of sugar
1 tablespoon chilli powder   2 tablespoons oil

Ingredients for the Seasoning

2 –3 dry chillies   ½ teaspoon mustard seeds
½ teaspoon black gram (urad dal)   5 to 6 curry leaves
½ teaspoon split chick peas   2 tablespoons oil
   (chana dal)

Method:

1. Heat oil in a wok. Add the onions and fry till it becomes transparent and slightly brown.
2. Add the tomatoes, fry till the tomatoes soften and keep aside for 2 minutes.
3. Then blend the onion and tomatoes to a fine paste.
4. Use the same wok to do your seasoning. Heat a little oil and add in the seasoning ingredients. Once the mustard seeds begin to crackle, pour the seasoning into the onion tomato paste.
5. Stir well and add salt, sugar and chilli powder.
6. Let it to simmer for 2 minutes.

The chutney is ready to be eaten with thosai or any kind of Indian or Western bread.

TOMATO PACHADI

Ingredients

3 to 4 tomatoes

7 to 8 green chillies

1 capsicum

tamarind juice (1 lemon size
  ball mixed with 2 glasses
  of water)

¼ teaspoon cumin seeds

¼ teaspoon mustard seeds

¼ teaspoon black gram (urad
  dal)

¼ teaspoon split chick peas
  (chana dal)

a pinch of asafoetida

¼ teaspoon turmeric powder

salt to taste

½ teaspoon sugar

Method:

1. Heat oil in a wok and add the cumin seeds, mustard seeds, split chick peas, black gram and asafoetida.
2. Then add the capsicum and chopped chillies.
3. Once the chillies have turned to a darker green, add the tomatoes.
4. Fry till the tomatoes become soft.
5. Add the tamarind juice, turmeric powder, chilli powder, salt and sugar
6. Let it boil for 5 minutes on medium heat.
7. Add more salt and sugar if the pachadi is too spicy.
8. Let it simmer for 2 minutes on medium heat.

The pachadi can be served with rice, thosai or chappati.

BUTTER MILK CURRY (MOORU KOLUMBU)

This dish is similar to the North Indian "Khadi" popular in Gujarat and Punjab.

Ingredients

vegetables of your choice	1 teaspoon cumin seeds
1 cup grated coconut	1 big tomato
2 green chillies	2 glasses yoghurt
2 pieces dry chillies	salt to taste

Ingredients for the Seasoning

½ teaspoon mustard seeds	5-6 curry leaves
¼ teaspoon fenugreek seeds	¼ teaspoon turmeric powder

You may use a choice of vegetables for this dish-potatoes, raw banana or okra. If you decide to use okra (about 4 to 5 pieces) then cut them in threes and deep fry them till they become slightly brown. Drain the excess oil and keep aside.

Method:

1. Take a medium sized pot and add about 1½ glasses of water. Add the tomatoes, turmeric powder, salt (about ½ teaspoon first) and your choice of vegetables. Let it simmer on medium heat.
2. While the vegetables are being cooked, grind the coconut, green chillies, dry chillies and cumin seeds with a little water

first to make it into a thick smooth paste. Add the yoghurt to the paste and grind again for ½ a minute. Keep aside.

3. Once the vegetables are cooked, turn off the stove and let the mixture cool for 2 minutes before adding the ground paste of coconut with yoghurt. (note: the yoghurt in the pot may separate if the vegetables are too hot)

4. Heat a little oil in a small frying pan and add in the seasoning ingredients. Once the mustard seeds begin to crackle, add it into the pot with vegetables and yogurt mix.

5. You may add a pinch of sugar if the curry is too sour. Also add more salt if required.

6. Simmer for one minute over a low flame before serving.

Note:

The yoghurt used for this dish should be sour. A piece of sour mango while boiling the vegetables or ¼ teaspoon dry mango powder (amchur powder) can also achieve the right level of flavour.

OKRA PACHADI (VENDAKKAI PACHADI)

Ingredients

6 okra

2 –3 dry chillies

1 tomato, chopped small

½ teaspoon black gram (urad dal)

½ teaspoon split chick peas (chana dal)

½ teaspoon mustard seeds

¼ teaspoon fenugreek seeds

a pinch of asafoetida

tamarind juice (lemon size ball, mixed with 1 glass of water)

¼ teaspoon turmeric powder

½ teaspoon chilli powder

salt to taste

2 tablespoons of oil

Method:

1. Wash and dry the okra. Cut them into thin slices. (about 5 mm thick)
2. Take the wok and heat the oil. Add mustard seeds and chillies. Wait till the mustard seeds begin to crackle.
3. Add black gram, fenugreek seeds, asafoetida and split chick peas dal (chana dal).
4. Fry for about half a minute then add the okra and tomato. Fry till tomato softens.
5. Add the tamarind juice, chilli powder, salt and turmeric powder. Mix well.
6. Boil for 5 minutes and the pachadi is done.

Note: If the pachadi is too sour for you, you may add a pinch of refined sugar or brown sugar.

I also would like to share a very interesting article that I came across in a leading women's magazine –A study shows that elderly folks in India have the lowest rate of Alzheimer's disease in the world, and researchers say this is due to the power of curcumin, the powerful compound found in turmeric.

It also says that low doses of curcumin blocks the accumulation of plaques and also reduce inflammation. Therefore it encourages you to increase from ¼ teaspoon to ½ teaspoon of turmeric powder in your curry or rice.

Therefore a good dose of turmeric everyday keeps Alzheimer's disease away!

CHETTINAD KOLUMBU

Ingredients

2 big potatoes

2 brinjals (eggplant)

4 okra

2 big tomatoes

2 big onions (or 6 shallots)

1 cinnamon stick

4 tablespoons curry powder

1 tablespoon fennel seeds
  (varyali)

6 – 8 pips garlic

12 to 15 pieces bird's eye
  chilli (cut into halves)

salt to taste

10 curry leaves

3 tablespoons of oil

tamarind juice (1 lemon
  size ball mixed with 2 ½
  glasses of water)

Method:

1. Mix the tamarind juice with the curry powder and keep aside.
2. Roast the cinnamon stick and fennel seeds together until fragrant and grind the mix into a fine powder and keep aside.
3. Heat oil in a wok and add the onions and garlic.
4. Once the onion is slightly brown, add all the vegetables and fry for 2 minutes.
5. Add tamarind juice mix, salt and curry leaves and boil till vegetables are well cooked.
6. Add the cinnamon-fennel powder and simmer for another 2 minutes.

The Chettinad Kolumbu is ready to be served with rice.

Note:

The vegetables are to be cut into chunks/quarters. The vegetables can also be deep fried first to enhance the taste. If this is the case, then vegetables should be added only after step 5.

SPICY BUTTERMILK (KARACHA MOORU)

This is an ideal drink on a hot day.

Ingredients

2 green chillies
a bunch of curry leaves
a bunch of coriander leaves
½ inch ginger
salt to taste
3 big ladles of yoghurt

Method:

1. First blend all the above ingredients except yoghurt with half a glass of water. Blend till mixture is a fine paste.
2. Sieve the paste and separate the juice from the pulp. Sieve half cup water through the pulp to extract more juice.
3. Now rinse the blender, add in the yoghurt and extracted juice. Blend for 20 seconds. Taste the buttermilk and add more salt if required.
4. The buttermilk is best served after chilling for 2 hours.

SOUTH INDIAN CREPE/PANCAKE (THOSAI)

The thosai (also known as Dosa) is possibly the most famous South Indian dish. This recipe gives the measurement for 2 persons, with 4 to 5 thosai each. Knowing how to make the thosai mix also opens the door to other variant snacks like "Masala Thosai", the "Onion Thosai" and even the "Oothappam"

Ingredients

1 ½ cup par boiled rice
½ cup uncooked white rice
1 teaspoon fenugreek seeds
¾ cup split peas dal (urad dal)

1. Soak the parboiled rice, white rice, fenugreek seeds and urad dal overnight. The urad dhal needs to be soaked separately.
2. In the morning, grind the urad dhal first. Remove the ground paste and put it in a big pot. Then put the rest of the ingredients into the blender and grind to a smooth batter. Remember not to add too much water.
3. Pour the batter into the big pot (with at least half the space to spare). Add 1 tablespoon of salt and mix well. Allow the batter to ferment. The batter should rise by evening.
4. Add more salt if required once the batter has fermented. You need to add about ¼ cup of water to the batter before using it.
5. Spread one ladle of batter evenly over the flat nonstick pan (tava). Use the bottom of the ladle to spread the batter with a

circular motion to form a pancake. You can make the thosai thick or thin as per your liking.

6. Turn the thosai over to cook on both sides. Use sesame seed oil (gingelly oil) for roasting on both sides for the best taste. Any other edible oil can also be used.

Serve with sambar, chutney or pachadi.

Make sure you have a separate tava (or non—stick pan) for the thosai. Don't mix it with the chapatti tava. The Thosai usually comes out smoothly only after the 3rd thosai is done. So don't give up easily.

Make sure you also wipe the hot tava with a cloth or onion dipped in oil in between every thosai for the best results.

ASIAN/WESTERN
MAIN COURSES

While Indian cooking offers a wide variety, I sometimes yearn for a different taste. In this section, I have included some "non-Indian" dishes which my family enjoys. I have even tried some of these dishes successfully on my in-laws, who are fairly conservative in their taste.

VEGETARIAN LASAGNA

Main Ingredients

2 onions, chopped small
1 pip garlic
1 carrot, chopped into small
    pieces
250g spinach, chopped small
1 packet fresh mushroom,
    chopped small
1 big tin of canned tomatoes,
    chopped small
2 tablespoons tomato puree

1 cube of vegetable stock,
    dissolve in 300 ml hot
    water
¼ teaspoon pepper powder
½ teaspoon turmeric powder
½ teaspoon chilli powder
lasagna sheets
50 g Parmesan cheese
salt to taste
2 tablespoons oil

Ingredients for Cheese Sauce:

4 tablespoons butter
8 tablespoons plain flour
800 ml milk
A pinch of nutmeg
50g of grated Cheddar cheese

METHOD:

Main filling:

1. Heat the oil in large pan and fry the onion, garlic, carrot and
   mushrooms for 4 to 5 minutes.

2. Add spinach and fry for another 4 minutes.
3. Put in tomatoes, puree, stock, salt, pepper, turmeric powder and chilli powder and simmer for 20 minutes.

In the meantime prepare the *Cheese sauce*:

1. Melt butter in a pan and then add the plain flour. Stir for 1 minute.
2. Turn off the stove and add milk slowly.
3. Turn on the stove again and stir the mixture until it thickens.
4. Add nutmeg and grated cheese, stir for 1 minute and keep aside.

To assemble the lasagna:

1. Preheat oven to 180 ^{0} c.
2. Put the lasagna sheet in a tray.
3. Pour a layer of main sauce and alternate with lasagna sheets till the main sauce and lasagna sheets finish.
4. Make sure the top layer is a lasagna sheet. Pour the cheese sauce and the Parmesan cheese on the top layer and bake for 30 to 45 minutes.

ASSAM PEDAS

Ingredients

Assam Pedas paste:
4 cloves garlic
6 shallots
½ inch fresh turmeric
2 stalks lemon grass
½ inch ginger
2 candle nuts (buah keras)
10 pieces bird eye chilli

Vegetables required:
1 eggplant, chopped big
4 okra, halved
2 big tofu, cut into 8 pieces

Other Ingredients:

40 g tamarind mixed with 2
   cups water and strained.
2 tablespoons dried red chilli
   paste

1 tablespoon sugar
salt to taste
4 tablespoons oil

Method:

1. Deep fry the vegetables and tofu and keep aside.
2. Prepare the assam pedas paste by grinding all the ingredients into a thick paste using only a little water.
3. Heat oil in a deep wok and add the ground paste. Fry for 5 minutes until oil separates.

4. Add chilli paste. Fry for another three minutes over a medium flame. Stir constantly to ensure the paste does not burn.
5. Add tamarind juice, salt and sugar and bring it to boil.
6. Add the fried vegetables and boil the curry on high flame till it thickens.
7. Taste the curry. Adjust the heat/spice to your liking.
8. Boil for another 2 minutes over a low flame and curry is ready to serve with rice.

VEGETARIAN MUTTON CURRY

Ingredients

1 potato, cubed and deep fried

3 okra, cut into halves and
   deep fried

250g vegetarian mutton,
   shallow fry for 30 second

1 cinnamon stick

1 tablespoon ginger garlic paste

2 big onions, chopped small

1 tablespoon chilli paste

2 tablespoons Baba's curry
   powder

¼ teaspoon sugar

1 glass coconut milk (santan)

1 tablespoon tamarind juice

5 curry leaves

¼ cup water

2 tablespoons oil

salt to taste

This recipe uses "vegetarian mutton" which is soya based and looks like the real thing. It is totally vegetarian and is used widely in Buddhist vegetarian cuisine. Most Indian and Asian grocery stores sell this item.

Method:

1. Heat oil in a wok and add the cinnamon stick, ginger garlic paste and onions.
2. Once the onions are transparent and slightly brown, add the chilli paste and cook for 3 minutes.
3. Add the vegetarian mutton and curry powder. (I prefer to use Baba's brand)
4. Mix well and cook for another 3 minutes.

5. Add the tamarind juice, salt, sugar and water. Boil for 4 minutes over a medium flame.
6. Add the coconut milk at this point. Also add in the fried okra and potatoes. Simmer for another 2 minutes.
7. Once done garnish with curry leaves.

DESSERT

No meal, irrespective of where in the world it is served is complete, without a dessert. India is famous for its variety of sweets in its cuisine. Each part of India is famous for a sweet dish, from the "Thirunalveli Halwa" and the "Mysore Pak" in the south to the "Firni", the "Jalebi" and the "Rasgollas" up north.

In this section, I have given the recipes for a few sweet dishes that are easy to prepare and good to eat.

SUJI PUDDING

Ingredients

1 cup wheat flour (Atta)
1 ½ cups clarified butter (ghee)
½ cup sugar
1 cup milk

A few chopped almonds, roasted with a little clarified butter till crunchy

Method:

1. Heat ghee in the wok. Then add in the wheat flour.
2. Keep stirring over a low flame for 10 minutes.
3. Once it changes colour to a darker brown, add in the sugar and milk and keep on stirring.
4. Once the mixture thickens, add in the chopped almonds. Mix it well and continue stirring for 2 minutes. Turn off the stove and remove wok from the stove.
5. Serve it warm to your guests.

VARSHA S. PATEL

THE KING OF ICE CREAMS — KULFI

Ingredients

1 litre full cream milk
1 small tin of condensed milk
½ cup grated nuts or unsalted pistachios
2 – 3 cardamom pods (elachi)

Method:

1. Bring milk to a boil in a heavy bottom pan and continue to boil for 10 minutes.
2. Add the condensed milk, nuts and cardamom pods and continue to boil it for another 15 minutes.
3. Turn off the gas and pour the liquid into individual serving bowls and cool to room temperature.
4. Chill the serving bowls in the freezer for around 8 hours before serving.

GULAB JAMUN (DUMPLINGS IN SUGAR SYRUP)

Ingredients

2 cups milk powder
1 cup self raising flour
1 small box thickened cream
oil/clarified butter (ghee) for
    deep frying

For the sugar syrup:
1 cup water
2 cups sugar
2 to 3 cardamom pods
Yellow colouring (optional)

Method:

1. Mix water, sugar and cardamom pods in a pot and heat liquid until it thickens into a syrup. Switch off the stove and add the colouring if desired then keep aside.
2. Mix the milk powder and self-raising flour in another bowl. Keep adding the thickened cream (spoon by spoon) till a soft dough is formed. Make round balls roughly 30mm in diameter and keep aside.
3. Heat oil in a large wok. Once the oil is hot, drop 5 to 6 balls at a time. Fry them on a low heat so that the inside gets cooked evenly. Fry until the balls are a dark golden colour. Remove from oil, and let the balls cool down for few minutes on a paper towel before transferring them into the sugar syrup. Leave the flour balls in the syrup for at least 2 hours.
4. You can serve the dumplings (Gulab Jamun) warm or cold to your guests.

EGGLESS CHOCOLATE CAKE

Ingredients

250 g butter

1 tin condensed milk

2 tablespoons sugar

½ can of Sprite/7 Up

2 tablespoons yoghurt

2 cups self-raising flour

½ cup cocoa powder

1 teaspoon vanilla essence

Method:

1. Preheat oven to 180 ^{0}C.
2. Beat butter, sugar and condensed milk together till the mixture is fluffy and light.
3. Now add the yoghurt, sprite and vanilla essence. Mix well.
4. Next add the flour and cocoa powder and beat till the mixture becomes a smooth texture.
5. Grease the cake pan lightly and pour mixture into it.
6. Bake for 30 to 40 minutes.
7. Use a skewer to check whether the cake is done. The skewer should come out clean without anything sticking to it.

ACKNOWLEDGEMENT

When I started out my married life, with no experience in cooking, I would never have dared to imagine that one day I would be writing a cookbook!

I would like to take this opportunity to thank:

> ➢ My family, who had the courage to eat what I cooked, and even more courage to tell me what they really thought!

> ➢ My sisters-in-law from both sides – Aruna, Suganthi and Ranjani—who have been my friends and an unending source of support. This book would not be a reality without them.

> ➢ My mother and my mother-in-law, who have given me standards to aspire to, and whose patience has culminated in this effort.

> ➢ I would also like to thank my husband Suresh for his input and helping me to edit and compile all the recipes.

> ➢ I dedicate this collection to my daughter Sanjana. Cooking for her is a daily challenge. She is my inspiration, my loudest critic and my greatest admirer.

GLOSSARY

One of the problems that I face with many cookbooks is that the names of the ingredients are given in the English language and often I face a lot of problems in matching these to the more familiar Indian names. I have managed to compile a glossary of these terms over the years in Hindi and Tamil, which I hope will be helpful to readers.

ENGLISH	HINDI	TAMIL
All Purpose Flour	Maida	Maida Maavu
Asafoetida	Hing	Perungayam
Banana	Kela	Vaazhai Palam
Black gram	Urad Dal	Ulundhu Paruppu
Butter	Makhan	Vaenai
Butter Milk	Chaas	Mooru
Cardamom	Elaichi	Ellakaai
Carrot	Gajar	Sivappu Mulangi
Cashew nuts	Kaju	Mundhiri Parupu
Cauliflower	Gobi	Poo kos
Chick Pea Flour	Besan	Kadalai Maavu
Chillies	Mirchi	Pattamilagai
Cinnamon	Dalchini	Pattai
Clarified Butter	Ghee	Nyei
Cloves	Lavang	Kirambu
Coconut	Nariyal	Thaengai
Coriander	Dhania	Kothamalli
Cucumber	Kakari	Velarikaai
Cumin	Jeera	Jeeragam
Dried mango powder	Amchur	Mangai Thool
Egg	Anda	Muttai
Eggplant/Brinjal	Baingan	KathiriKaai

Fennel	Saunf/Varyali	Soombhu
Fenugreek	Methi	Mendhayam
Garlic	Lahsun	Poondu
Ginger	Adrak	Inji
Green Gram	Moong dal	Paasi Paruppu
Ground nuts	Moongphali	Vaer Kadalai
Honey	Madhu	Thaen
Jaggery/Brown Sugar	Gur	Karumbu Sarkarai
Lady's fingers/Okra	Bhindi	Vendakaai
Lemon	Nimbu	Yaelumichai
Mango	Aam	Maangai
Milk	Doodh	Paal
Mustard Seeds	Sarson/Rai	Kadugu
Nutmeg	Jaiphal	Jaathikaai
Oil	Tel	Ennai
Onions	Piaz	Vaengayam
Peas	Matar	Pataani
Pepper	Kali mirch	Milagu
Pickles	Achar	Oorugaai
Pigeon Peas	Toor Dal	Thoovaram Paruppu
Potato	Aloo	Uralai Kilangu
Pulses	Dal	Paruppu
Radish	Mooli	Mulanki
Red chilli	Lal mirch	Milakai Thool
Rice	Chawal	Arrisi
Saffron	Kesar	Kunkuma Poo
Salt	Namak	Uppu
Semolina	Sooji	Ravai
Split Chick Peas	Channa Dal	Kadalai Paruppu
Sugar	Chini	Sarkarai
Tamarind	Imli	Puli
Thickened Milk	Mawa	Paal Kova
Tomato	Tamatar	Thakaali
Turmeric	Haldi	Manjal
Wheat	Gehun	Godhumai

Wheat Flour	Atta	Godhumai Maavu
White Chick Peas	Kabuli Chana	Kondai Kadalai
Yoghurt	Dahi	Thayir

In all the recipes in my book, I have not given the measurement for salt as I find it is up to the individual requirement.